The Survival Tin: The Survival Kit You Can Carry in Your Pocket

by M. Anderson

I0411361

Disclaimer:

The information contained in this book is for general information purposes only. This book is sold with the understanding the author and/or publisher is not giving medical advice, nor should the information contained in this book replace medical advice, nor is it intended to diagnose or treat any disease, illness or other medical condition.

While we endeavor to keep the information up to date and correct, we make no representations or warranties of any kind, express or implied, about the completeness, accuracy, reliability, suitability or availability with respect to the book or the information, products, services, or related graphics contained book for any purpose. Any reliance you place on such information is therefore strictly at your own risk.

Dedication:

This book is dedicated to my loving wife, who's had to deal with my obsession with backyard chickens, survival skills and homesteading for many long years. I love you sweetie! Thanks for being so understanding.

Contents

The Survival Tin

A survival tin is a mini-survival kit you can carry into the field in your pocket. You fill it with the small tools and supplies that you're most likely to need in an emergency situation. It's designed to be carried on your person, so you'll always have it with you when it's needed.

The term "survival tin" is used to refer to any small container a person uses to carry survival gear. Film canisters, metal tins, plastic cases and even tobacco pouches have all been used as "tins." While any small container that can be placed in your pocket will suffice, the most common tin used as a survival tin is the Altoids tin. This has led to the survival tin being nicknamed the BOAT, which is an acronym for "Bug Out Altoids Tin."

The container itself doesn't matter. It's what you put in it that counts.

The items you put into your tin should be the items you think you're most likely to need in an emergency situation. Most preppers build their tin with the thought of using the contents in it to help them get back home if they're caught out and about when disaster strikes. The tin isn't designed to help them survive over an extended period of time; the intent is to help them survive the day or two it takes to get home on foot, if need be.

Carrying a survival tin instead of a bulky bag allows you to blend into the crowd in an emergency situation. It also allows you to carry survival gear into places you normally wouldn't feel comfortable or be allowed to carry a bag of gear. It's still a good idea to keep a Get Home Bag in your car or your locker at work. The survival tin is designed to protect you in case you get separated from your Get Home Bag and can't get to it or are out somewhere without your bag.

What's in a Kit?

The best survival tins contain items that cover each of your basic needs in an emergency. There are 8 common categories of items contained in a survival tin:

- **Fire.**
- **First aid.**
- **Food and Water.**
- **Information.**
- **Light.**
- **Miscellaneous.**
- **Navigation.**
- **Signaling.**

It's recommended you try to cover each of these categories the best you can. Since space is limited, you're going to be limited to one or two items per category—and they're going to have to be small.

Who Should Carry One?

A good mini-survival kit is something everyone should carry with them when they leave the house. If you step out of your door to do more than walk around the block, you should have your survival kit in your pocket. The day you leave your house without your kit will be the day you end up needing it. It never fails.

Your kit is your insurance policy against the many curveballs life can throw you. If there's a disaster or crisis situation, you may be forced to survive on just the contents of your kit. Having a well-built kit drastically ups your odds of survival. If you're caught without one, the odds are against you.

Don't plan on being able to buy your way home.

In a bad enough emergency, stores will be closed and public transportation will either be nonexistent or extremely limited. There's a good chance your plastic cards will be worthless, and there's the possibility that cash money might not be accepted. You could be left with the contents of your tin as the only thing standing between you and a world of hurt.

Survival tins aren't just for the grown men in the family.

Women and children traveling away from home should carry them, too. Woman should carry kits that are small enough to be carried outside their purse. In a true emergency situation, they may need to ditch the bulky purse and strike off without it. Carrying a purse may make them an easy target in a situation where rule of law has been suspended.

If your children are allowed to leave the house without supervision, they should be required to carry a survival kit with them.

Responsible older children and teens may carry similar kits to what the adults carry. For younger children, you may want to eliminate the matches, blades and other destructive objects. You don't want to have to explain to an officer of the law that the pile of leaves your kids just set on fire and pushed down the slide at the park was created from matches they got from a "survival kit" you gave them.

The Container

What you use as a container for your survival tin is up to you. Whatever you decide on, it should be portable and able to be tucked away in one of your pockets. Those are the only real "rules" when it comes to survival tins.

You're going to be carrying your tin with you wherever you go, so keep that in mind when choosing the container. Pick something too bulky and you aren't going to be able to carry it with you when you're wearing something with small pockets. You'll be able to fit more stuff into a larger container, but who wants to carry something the size of a coffee can with them everywhere they go?

The most common container used for survival tins is the metal Altoid tin. Here are the dimensions of the tin:

3.7" x 2.3" x 0.8"

This gives you just under 7 cubic inches of storage space in which to pack your supplies.

You can buy a pack of Altoids to get the tin, or you can buy tins that are a similar size online. There are a number of different colors of tins available, ranging from unpainted metal to urban camouflage. I'm of the opinion that the best urban camouflage is the unaltered Altoids tin. It looks like a tin of tasty breath mints, but contains gear that'll save a lot more than your breath.

Think about it for a second.

If you're in an emergency situation and are desperate for supplies, would you be more likely to notice a person who pulls out a can of breath mints or a person who pulls out a tin painted in urban camo? The camo tin isn't going to blend in with its surroundings. It's going to stick out like a sore thumb. The unpainted tins are going to be even more obvious because they're going to reflect sunlight and draw attention every time you take the tin out of your pocket.

The only benefit I see to buying one of the unpainted tins is that you can get larger tins that will hold more gear. There are even tins that come with a belt pouch, so you don't have to carry them in your pocket, which might be a good option for those who prefer pants so tight they have to use a pry bar to get them on.

Survival tins aren't just made of tin.

There are a number of other options available for those who want to be different. Here are some of the other items people are using to store their mini-survival kits:

- **Film canisters.** While film canisters are small and easy to carry, you're going to have to pack light. A 35mm canister has a volume of around 3 cubic inches. That's less than half of what a breath mint tin will hold. There are screw-top vials sold that will hold more than the average film canister.
- **Otterbox waterproof cases.** These little boxes are practically indestructible. They're also waterproof and many of them come with a foam liner that will protect your gear.

- **Pouches.** There are a number of pouches and bags that can be filled with gear and tossed in your pocket. They're often puncture-resistant and waterproof, but don't offer much protection for your gear.

- **Sardine can.** There's a survival kit sold that's packed into a sardine can. It has a tab that you pull to remove the lid. There's at least one huge problem with this kit. Once you pop the top on the can, what do you do with your stuff? The lid appears to be one-time use only, which leads me to believe this kit is more of a novelty than it is a functional survival kit.

- **Screw-top tins.** These tins are round and have lids that are screwed onto them. Split shots for fishing and pellets for pellet guns are commonly sold in these tins. Steer clear of the round tins with the lids that have to be pressed on. They don't seal up tightly and will come off, spilling the contents of the tin into your pocket.

- **Scuba capsules.** These handy little capsules come complete with key rings that allow you to hang them from your keychain. They tend to run a bit small, so it might take a couple of them to hold your gear.

- **Sports cases.** These handy cases can be worn around your neck or thrown in your pocket. They're designed for athletes to use to keep credit cards, business cards and cash safe and dry, but they also work well as survival tins. They have the added bonus of being waterproof, which is something breath mint tins definitely aren't.

- **Tobacco pouches.** This one might sound a little strange, but it's the ultimate in urban camo. Nobody would expect a survival kit to be stored in a tobacco pouch.

The reality is the container doesn't matter nearly as much as what you put into it. Choose the container you're most likely to carry on you on a daily basis. A survival tin isn't going to do you much good sitting on your dresser at home.

Fire: The True Multitool

Fire is one of the most valuable tools you can have in an emergency situation. It's the true "multitool" in your survival tin. Fire can be used for the following survival purposes:

- **Cauterizing wounds.**
- **Clearing brush.**
- **Cooking food.**
- **Creating a torch.**
- **Defensive purposes.**
- **Drying wet clothes and gear.**
- **Hardening the points of wooden spears and arrows.**
- **Heat.**
- **Light.**
- **Making charcoal.**
- **Sanitizing water.**
- **Signaling.**
- **Smoking food and hides.**
- **Smoking small game out of their holes.**
- **Warding off predators.**

I'm sure I've left a few items off the list, but you get the point. Fire is an absolute necessity when it comes to survival. You're going to need fire to stay alive, especially if you're stuck out in the cold.

While you obviously can't carry a flaming piece of wood around in your pocket, you can carry tools that allow you to start a fire. I recommend carrying at least 2 fire-starting tools with you in your kit.

Here are some of the more common fire-starting tools people carry in their survival tins:

- **Battery and steel wool.** A 9-volt battery and steel wool can be used to start a fire. Twist up a small piece of steel wool and touch it to both the positive and negative terminals on the battery. The steel wool will light up quickly. Drop it into some tender and stoke a flame. Don't hold the steel wool with your bare fingers when you're lighting it.
- **Butane torch.** A torch is a great source of fire as long as it has fuel. You might have room for a small butane lighter in your kit, but you won't be able to bring along extra fuel. This is a good source of flame, but shouldn't be your only source of flame.
- **Magnesium fire starter and striker.** Everybody should have one of these in their kit. The smaller ones won't take up much space and they can be used to start hundreds of fires. Make sure you practice starting fires with them in advance. There's a bit of a learning curve and you don't want to try to learn as you're shivering in the cold.
- **Magnifying glass.** You can use a magnifying glass to focus sunlight on a piece of tinder to set it on fire. The downside to relying on this method is it only works on a sunny day.

- **Matches.** I know a lot of people carry matches in their kits. The problem with matches is you aren't going to be able to carry a lot of them and they're one-time-use only. If you do decide to carry a few matches, lifeboat matches are your best bet. They're covered with a combustible compound and are waterproof. These matches will continue to burn even if there's a good breeze blowing. You don't want to start with 5 matches and have 3 of them blow out before you get your fire started.

- **String.** You can make a bow and drill out of string, a piece of wood and a relatively straight stick. Use the bow to create friction between the stick and the piece of wood. This is the hardest method of starting a fire, but is one any true survivalist should be well-practiced in. You should have string (or paracord) in your survival tin anyway. You should know how to use it to make fire.

In addition to fire-starting tools, you're going to need tinder to help get your fire started. Tinder is highly flammable material that lights up easily. You use it to get your fire started. Many of the tools in the previous list won't work without tinder.

Here are some items you can include in your tin that can be used as tinder:

- **Dryer lint.** Cotton dryer lint is extremely flammable as long as it's kept dry. In a pinch, you can collect it from the bottoms of your pockets and use it to start a fire. Try coating the lint with paraffin wax for even better tinder that burns longer.

- **Wood shavings.** You can use bark or wood shavings as tinder. Light woods like birch, juniper or cedar work best. When collecting shavings for tinder, cut them as thin as possible and rub them between your fingers to puff them out. While you probably aren't going to want to carry bark or wood shavings in your kit, it's good to know they can be used as tinder.
- **Cotton ball and petroleum jelly.** Cover a cotton ball in petroleum jelly and you have a fire source that will burn for quite some time when you touch it off with some sparks or a flame.
- **Cattails.** The fluffy insides of cattails can be used as tinder. Rub the cattail between your fingers until it fluffs out and create a nest out of the fluff. You aren't going to carry a cattail in your survival tin, but you might stumble across a lake, river or marsh that has them growing along the banks and be able to grab a couple.
- **Perfume sample cards.** Those little cards that sit by the perfume bottles in department stores make great tinder. Look for the cards that are made from fibrous paper for best results. I like to dip my cards in melted paraffin wax to make them even more effective. These are one of the best choices for a survival tin because you can throw 3 or 4 of them in your tin and not take

much of a hit as far as space is concerned. Each card can be torn into pieces that can be used to light multiple fires.

- **Sawdust and paraffin wax.** Mix sawdust and melted paraffin on a cookie sheet and spread it out so it's flat. Let it cool and cut into 1-inch squares. These burn hot and can easily be used to start a fire.
- **Steel wool.** Steel wool ignites easily and can be fluffed out and used as tinder. It can be ignited using a 9-volt battery (or any battery, for that matter) or it can be ignited by using a fire starter to throw sparks on it.
- **Twine.** Cotton twine can be unraveled and used as tinder.
- **Tampons.** Tampons can be used to make tinder. In fact, these are one of the better choices for survival tin tinder because there are tons of ways you can use tampons in a survival situation. To use it as tinder, pick off a little bit of the cotton material and fluff it up. The compressed "bullet" size tampons are a great addition to your kit.

Whatever you do, don't throw a book of regular matches in your tin and call it good.

Fire is one of the most important tools you have when it comes to survival. You're going to want to have multiple means of creating fire, ample tinder to get your fires started and the knowledge required to start fires using the tools you include in your kit.

The more you practice at home when your life doesn't depend on getting the fire started; the better off you'll be in a life and death situation. A crisis situation shouldn't be the first time you try to build fire with your fire starting tools.

Practice makes perfect and you can't afford to waste supplies practicing in an emergency.

First Aid: Choose Your Items Wisely

Considering the fact that average first aid kits contain hundreds of items, you're going to feel severely limited when it comes to the items you're able to fit into your survival tin. You could fill the entire tin with first aid items only and still not feel completely at ease.

The first and most important items you're going to want to include in your kit is at least a 3-day supply of any prescription medications you take. Drugstores and pharmacies could be closed and you may not be able to make it home to your meds for a few days if you have to walk. Keeping a few of each of your meds will help ensure your body is functioning at maximum capacity. You may end up having to walk long distances and maybe even run. You're going to be asking a lot of your body. Not having your prescription medications can place an added load on your already stressed system—and it does so at a time when medical care may be nonexistent.

You're going to want to be care for cuts, burns and other wounds to keep them from getting infected. Add a few adhesive bandages to cover the minor injuries. A couple butterfly bandages will allow you to seal off deeper cuts. I'd also toss in a needle and some thread, so you can sew up deeper cuts. Make sure you properly clean your wounds before sewing them up to help prevent infection. A couple packets of Neosporin can be used to help fight off infection.

Superglue can also be used to seal cuts in the field. Don't use it in deep cuts because some types of super glue create heat as they create the bond and can kill tissue in the process. Butyl-cyanoacrylate is medical superglue used by veterinarians to seal animal wounds, but it hasn't been approved for use on humans. You can get a small tube of it online for around $20 in case your, uh, pets need to be patched up. Skin irritation and infection can occur when using superglue, so be careful and don't use it on deep wounds.

We talked about tampons in the section on fire. They're also useful when it comes to deep injuries like gunshot wounds. You can place a tampon in a bullet wound to help stop the bleeding until you can get professional help. You can also place tampons over injuries that are bleeding profusely to help stop the flow of blood.

When an artery is hit in one of your extremities, stopping the bleeding is of utmost importance. An injury to one of the bigger arteries in your body will cause you to bleed out in a matter of minutes if you don't stop the bleeding. One way to stop bleeding in the field is to make a tourniquet. While most tourniquets are too big to fit in a survival tin, you can include some twine or string and a metal or wooden dowel in your kit that can be used to create a makeshift tourniquet. Wrap the string around the limb above the injury and use the dowel to twist it tight until the bleeding stops. This isn't ideal, but may slow the bleeding enough to help you survive until you can get medical care.

Paracord works well for makeshift tourniquets. It's rather bulky and will take up quite a bit of space in your survival tin, but there are other ways to carry it with you. Paracord lanyards, bracelets and belts are all available. I recommend wearing one of the paracord belts because they give you the most bang for your buck. They hold your pants up most of the time, but can be unraveled to give you up to a hundred feet of paracord.

You can use a wooden pencil as your dowel. Cut it down to size to make it fit in your tin. This will give you a good dowel that serves double-duty as a writing utensil in case you need to jot down a note or two.

One note about using paracord as a tourniquet. It's not an ideal choice because it is too narrow and can cause tissue damage. You'll be better off using a piece of torn cloth or a standard tourniquet if available. That said, it's good to know you can use it if you absolutely have to.

There are two more items you can include in your kit that may be of use.

The first item is a pair of tweezers. Tweezers can be used to extract everything from bullet fragments to bee stingers and you'll be glad you have them if you have something stuck under your skin that you can't get out otherwise. They're a great precision tool that can be used to maneuver small parts into place. I'm partial to Uncle Bill's Sliver Gripper Tweezers, which are small, heavy-duty and easy to handle.

The second item is a scalpel blade or a surgical razor. Scalpel blades that have a point can be used to poke holes and make precise cuts. Surgical razors are easier to grip and have a wider blade. Or you can go all out and include a Derma-shave single edge razor. This handy blade is a folding scalpel that opens up to reveal a razor sharp blade that could be used as a weapon in a pinch. While it's compact, it'll take up more space in your kit than a scalpel blade or two, but it the benefit of having a larger blade with a handle may make it worth your while.

Food and Water: Or Should I Say Water and Food?

Ask most people the one item they can't live without and they'll tell you food is critical to survival. While it's true you'll eventually die without food, there are a number of documented cases of people going on hunger strikes for a month or longer. Mahatma Gandhi once went 21 days without food, only allowing himself a sip of water here and there.

Water, on the other hand, is something you won't live long without. You're going to need a source of clean water and you're going to need it fast. Estimates of how long a person can last without water vary widely, with some experts claiming you can die in as little as 48 hours, while others go on record stating you can last up to a week.

There are documented cases of people lasting more than a week without water, but the end result is usually death. Surviving that long without water doesn't mean you're going to survive once you're found. After anything more than a few days without water, the body goes into severe dehydration and medical attention is required to bring you back from the brink.

After a day without water, you're going to be miserable. Two days and you'll be suffering from headaches, stomachaches, dizziness, fainting and possibly hallucinations. Day three will see you suffering from lethargy as your mind and body slow down. You'll be walking around in a daze, unable to focus or think clearly. As your body temperature rises, you'll start shaking uncontrollably and may have seizures. If you last longer than three days, you'll be living a miserable existence. Every waking minute will be spent wishing you had something to drink. Eventually you'll fade away and die, as your heart or respiratory system will give out from the stress being placed on it.

While you can live without water for a few days, your survival may depend on your being able to think clearly. You won't be able to focus if you don't stay hydrated. You're going to need at least a couple liters of water a day; more if temperatures are high or you're exerting yourself physically.

Even if you filled your survival tin with water and nothing else, it would only hold enough water for a few sips. That would wet your mouth, but do little to hydrate you. So what can you do? Instead of carrying water, you're going to need to carry a way to disinfect potentially contaminated water. You can items with you that will allow you to decontaminate water so you can drink it. This will allow you to gather water from ponds, puddles and other water sources that you normally wouldn't drink from and make the water relatively safe to drink.

You're going to need something to hold water in, so you can carry it with you. An emergency water storage bag will allow you to carry up to a liter of water. When it isn't in use, it can be collapsed and folded up into a small square. Bigger bags that carry more than a liter are available, but these aren't good options for survival tins because they take up too much space.

You can also use condoms to store water. The bigger condoms can hold a gallon of water or more before they bust. Make sure you pack unlubricated condoms if you plan on using them to store water. Magnums will hold more water than most other brands. They'll also impress the ladies if they see the contents of your survival tin.

Once you've found water, you're going to need to filter and sterilize it. You can filter it through a piece of cloth like a sock or a bandana. This will get rid of any particulate matter floating in the water.

Drinking contaminated water can make you extremely ill and cause you to become more dehydrated than if you hadn't drank the water at all. Drink some truly bad water and you'll be losing fluid from diarrhea and vomiting faster than you can replace it. You don't want to take this risk when time is of essence.

One option for sterilizing water is to boil it.

Your kit should have multiple ways to make fire in it, so that part shouldn't be a problem. The problem lies in finding a container to boil the water in. You could use your tin; as long as you don't mind spending hours holding it over the fire when you could be traveling. This would work for a sip or two of water, but isn't a good option for someone trying to get home within a day or two. You're going to need something to boil larger amounts of water in if this is to be an effective method. Keep your eye out for a metal container. If you find one, you can use it to boil water in. Just be careful not to use metal contaminated with lead or some other poisonous substance.

You could end up opening yourself up to a world of hurt.

Aluminum foil can be folded up and added to your tin. You can create a cup out of your foil and use the cup you make to boil water in. It's going to be tough to include enough foil in your kit to make this worthwhile, but it's an option you can consider. There's conflicting information out there as to how well this works in a survival situation. If you fold the foil correctly it will work.

A better option for a survival tin built to help you survive a few days on your own is to include a handful of water purification tablets. You fill your water bag, drop a tablet (or part of a tablet, depending on how much water you have) into it and let it sit for the specified period of time. The tablets make the water safe to drink and you're able to gather water and keep on the move using this method.

Bleach will also work to disinfect water, but it would be tough to carry enough bleach to make it worth your while. I guess you could carry a small vial of bleach with you, but the purification tablets are easier to pack. If you do decide you want to carry bleach, use household bleach that has between 4% and 6% sodium hypochlorite and no additional additives like color savers or perfumes.

If the water you're drinking is clear, use a couple drops of bleach per liter of water. Let it sit for a half hour and smell the water. It should have the slight scent of chlorine. If it doesn't, add a couple more drops and let it sit for another half hour. For cloudy water, start with 4 drops of bleach.

A 2% solution of tincture of iodine can also be used. Add 5 drops of 2% tincture to each liter of water. If you decide to carry iodine, it has the additional benefit of being able to be used to disinfect wounds.

You're going to have the same problem with food that you do with water. You aren't going to be able to pack enough food to stave off hunger while you're trying to survive. Instead, you're going to have to pack items that can help you catch food.

There are a couple items people pack into their survival tins that can be used to obtain food. The first item is snare wire, which can be used to set traps to trap small game animals. There's only one problem with packing snare wire. It doesn't work unless you know how to set up proper snares. I mention this because I've run across a lot of people who have snare wire in their kits, but have no clue as to how to set a snare. I actually had a guy tell me he was planning on holding the snare wire and sitting really still until an animal walked into it, at which time he planned on pulling the snare tight and trapping the animal.

The right way to use a snare is to find a well-traveled game path and set the snare along the path. When an animal walks through the snare, the loop in the snare closes tight, trapping the animal in the snare. It helps to know what kind of animal it is you're planning on trapping because you need to have the snare set at the correct height and with the correct size loop.

To be completely honest with you, you can include snare wire because it can be used for a number of things, but the chance of you getting lucky and snaring an animal even if you set the snare correctly are pretty slim. If you plan on using snares to trap enough food to live on, you're going to need multiple snares along multiple paths. You aren't going to be able to pack enough wire to set up more than 1 or maybe 2 snares. You're also going to need time to wait for an animal to get caught and to circle around and check the snares you've set.

Snares work well in the woods where there's ample game. In an urban survival situation, there may not be enough game in the city to make it worth your while. That is, unless you don't mind surviving on cats, rats and the occasional raccoon or possum.

The second food-related item people pack into their survival tins is the fishing kit. Throw a few hooks, swivels and split shots of various sizes into a plastic baggy. Wrap 50 feet or so of fishing line around a small, flat piece of cardboard or a sewing bobbin and you've got your fishing kit. If you have room, you might want to throw in two bobbins with line on them—one with strong braided line that can be used to catch anything and the other with light line for smaller fish that are line shy. You can even toss in a few of your favorite small rubber fishing lures.

In the absence of lures, you can always find bugs to use as bait. Turn over a few rocks and you should be able to find something to use. You may be able to trap crawdads, minnows or tadpoles along the shoreline as well. If there's a dead animal close by, you can cut off a piece of it to use as catfish bait. The stinkier, the better. Catfish love smelly stuff.

Speaking of dead animals, you can use dead animals or dead fish you find along the shore to catch crawfish, which are a good source of food. Cut off a large chunk of meat and tie it or hook it to your fishing line. Find a good area to fish. If there's an area with murky water that looks like swamp water, that's probably where the crawdads will be. Drop the line in the water along the shore and wait for 5 to 10 minutes. Slowly lift the line out of the water. If you're lucky, there will be a crawdad or two latched onto it eating the fish. Continue to pull the line up slowly and grab the crawdad when it gets close enough. Be careful—the larger crawdads can give you a good pinch with their claws.

Again, fishing takes time, but it's probably a faster method of obtaining food than setting snares and waiting for something to walk into them, especially if you're only able to set a single snare. If you find a good body of water to fish, you may be able to catch dinner in a matter of minutes. All it takes is one good fish or a couple smaller fishes to make a meal.

Finding a place to fish in the city can sometimes be tough. Golf courses often have small ponds that are packed full of fish. You can also look for parks that have ponds or lakes that are normally off-limits. Drainage culverts that hold water year-round can be great places to fish, as can small streams that meander their way through town. If you have preplanned routes you plan on taking home, hop on Google Earth and use the satellite view to scout for bodies of water along the route. Even if you don't have a preplanned route, you can scout the city and identify potential fishing holes.

Be sure to physically check out your spots (and fish them, if legal) whenever possible, because the pictures on Google Earth can be old. You don't want to plan on having a fishing spot available to you only to get there and find out it's been filled in and turned into a housing tract. I recommend scouting your fishing spots at different times of the year to make sure they have water year-round. I hand-picked a small pond that looked perfect along one of my routes. I scouted it out and it looked great. A month later I came back to check it out again and it was empty. It turns out the pond gets drained a couple times a year. I could have wasted valuable time fishing this pond when there wasn't anything in there to catch.

When all else fails, get a handful of rocks and go pigeon hunting. Most cities are packed full of these birds, and the average person despises them, myself included. I tolerate them, though, because in an emergency, they'll make an almost endless supply of food. That is, until everyone else gets hungry and catches on.

Hopefully by then I'll be home to my stockpile.

Information: It's All In the Cards

There are two types of information you're going to want to carry in your kit:

- **Contact and identification information.**
- **Survival information.**

Contact and identification information should fit on a single credit card-sized card. You can type it out and print it or hand-write it; just make sure it's legible. You don't want to finally get to a location with cell phone service only to find you can't tell whether the third number is a 1, a 7 or a 4.

Contact information should include important phone numbers you might need to call in an emergency, as well as emergency contact names and numbers rescuers can call if they find you and you're incapacitated or didn't make it.

I recommend including the following information on your contact card:

- **Your cell and home phone number.**
- **Your home address.**
- **Your date of birth.**
- **Health insurance information.**
- **Blood type.**
- **Any health problems, allergies or concerns first responders might need to know.**
- **Prescription medications you're taking.**

- **Significant other's name, cell and home phone number.**
- **Parent's names, cell and home phone numbers.**
- **Children's names, ages, cell and home phone numbers.**
- **Other emergency contact's names, home and cell phone numbers.**
- **Police department phone numbers.**
- **Sheriff's department phone numbers.**
- **Highway patrol phone numbers.**
- **Fire department phone numbers.**
- **Local hospital phone numbers.**
- **Your doctor's phone number.**

I've seen some books and websites recommend you include your Social Security number as part of your identity information so you can easily be identified, but that's probably not the best idea. If you lose your card, you're opening yourself up to having your identity stolen.

In addition to contact numbers and personal information, all but the most practiced of survivalists are going to want to include a card or two that contains survival information on it. This is information you need to help you stay alive in a survival situation. This is especially important if you aren't well-practiced in survival, and let's face it, most of us aren't as practiced as we'd like to be.

Here's a list of information you might want to include on your card:

- **Basic first aid.**
- **How to make a fire.**
- **How to make a solar still.**
- **How to purify water.**
- **How to tie common knots.**
- **How to use your compass.**
- **How to use your signaling mirror.**
- **Making a shelter.**
- **Morse code.**
- **The fishing spots you scouted.**

You can make up a card or two yourself, or you can buy pre-made cards like the Brunton Emergency Pocket Survival Kit, which comes with three cards containing basic survival information.

Make sure you laminate your cards to waterproof them. You don't want to open your kit in the rain and have all of your information get reduced to a pile of wet pulp.

Light: Not Just for Seeing at Night

While lighting your path is one of its most important uses, light isn't just for seeing at night. It may be the only thing standing between you and a painful and/or violent death. You're going to need light to survive. It can be the difference between life and death.

Light can be used for the following things:

- **Attracting fish.**
- **Blinding enemy combatants.**
- **Causing game animals to freeze, making them easy targets.**
- **Maintaining high spirits.**
- **Scaring off predators.**
- **Seeing in the dark.**
- **Signaling search parties, especially at night.**

There aren't a whole lot of lights on the market that will fit in a survival tin. Most flashlights are way too big and bulky to toss in your tin. Even if you could find one that fits, it would be too heavy and would take up too much space.

Your only real option is to include a mini-LED light as part of your kit. These lights are small and light, and they have a relatively bright light for how small they are. Some of the better lights aren't much bigger than a quarter and produce a bright beam that will help you see at night and can be seen from a good distance away. There are lights available that have a strobe light mode designed to maximize your chances of being found if you're trying to signal for help. A steady light may blend into its surroundings and be missed. A pulsing or flashing light is tough to overlook.

Spend the extra money and get one of the good ones and you'll have a source of light that's built to last and will work for long periods of time on a single battery. You can throw an extra battery or two in your tin with very little impact on space.

Another option when it comes to light is fire.

You can use fire to light up your campsite at night to keep predators at bay. Animals will normally steer clear of a campsite with a fire lit. The only problem with using fire is it's tough to stay incognito with a fire burning. In an exposed area, your campfire can be seen for miles. If you want to fly under the radar, but need warmth or an open flame to cook food and boil water, try digging a hole and building your fire in the hole. The smoke from your fire will still be visible during the day, but if your hole is deep enough, your campfire will largely be hidden from sight.

You can also create a torch to carry with you at night to light your path. Here are the steps you need to follow to build a torch:

1. Find a thick branch or a large stick.
2. Wrap a piece of cloth around it. Alternatively, you can peel bark off of a tree and wrap it around the branch. You want to find trees with bark you can peel off in sheets. Use as combination of

green and dry bark to ensure your torch burns for as long as possible.

3. Bind the bark or cloth tightly to the branch.

4. Depending on the type of bark you used, you may need to stuff dry kindling into any gaps there are in the bark to get it to light and stay lit.

5. Light your torch. This type of torch will usually burn for a half hour to more than an hour if built correctly. Try adding animal fat or pine tar to it to keep it burning longer.

Miscellaneous: Other Items You Might Want to Add

This section outlines other items you might want to add to your survival tin. Please note that all of these items aren't going to fit in your tin at once. You're going to have to pick and choose the items that are most important to you.

Also keep in mind that some of the items listed may not be legal to carry in the area where you live. It's up to you to know what is and isn't legal in your jurisdiction. Don't e-mail me complaining that you got arrested because of something you had in your survival tin. I'm just putting the information out there. It's your responsibility to know the law and to make sure you don't run afoul of it.

Condoms

Toss an unlubricated condom that hasn't been treated with spermicide in your survival tin. These bad boys aren't just for safe sex, which will probably be the last thing on your mind in a survival situation.

Condoms can be used for the following purposes:

- **Water storage.** You can store a couple liters of water in a single large condom. Tie the top off to keep it from leaking out.
- **Store items inside them to keep them dry.**
- **Use as a fire accelerant.** Latex is highly flammable.
- **Fill with water and use as a magnifying glass to start a fire on a sunny day.**
- **Make a slingshot.**
- **Tie off tightly with an air bubble inside and use as a makeshift bobber.**
- **Use as a tourniquet.**
- **Fill up with air and tie it off to use it as a makeshift flotation device.**

Make sure you get standard thickness condoms. The ultrathin ones may feel better in the sack, but they aren't made to hold up in a survival situation.

Paperclips

When you're looking for items to put in your tin, you want small, useful items that aren't going to take up a lot of space. Paperclips are one such item. You're probably going to want to include a couple paperclips in your kit.

Here are some of the many uses for paperclips:

- **Bind small items together.**
- **Blowgun dart.**
- **Button replacement.**
- **Clean under your nails.**
- **Cotter pin.**
- **Emergency fuse replacement.**
- **Eyeglass repair.**
- **Fish hook.**
- **Hair clip.**
- **Let air out of tires.**
- **Replacement zipper pull.**
- **Stick in door locks and break off to slow down pursuers.**
- **Straighten it out and use it as a small splint.**
- **Unclog holes.**
- **Use to make a makeshift compass.**

Paracord

This was mentioned in the section on first aid. I'm also including it here because it can be used as so much more than a tourniquet.

Again, you aren't going to be able to include a lot of paracord in your tin because of its thickness. Wearing a necklace, belt or bracelet made of paracord is a better option because it will allow you to carry a lot more of this useful tool. Alternatively, you can wrap the paracord around the outside of your kit to save space inside. This will allow you to bring along as much paracord as you're comfortable fitting in your pocket.

Here are some of the uses of paracord:

- **Belt.**
- **Binding stuff together.**
- **Clothesline.**
- **Create a snare to trap small game.**
- **Creating a shelter by tying branches together.**
- **Creating splints and slings.**
- **Emergency tourniquet.**
- **Hang supplies to keep them out of the reach of animals.**
- **Life line.**
- **Loop it to create tow rope.**
- **Making weapons by tying sharp objects to sticks to create spears and arrows.**
- **Setting up trip wires.**
- **Shoe lace.**
- **Tying the hands of enemies.**

- **Unravel it and use the inner strands as fishing line.**
- **Unravel it and use the inner strands as floss.**
- **Unravel it and use the inner strands as thread.**

These are just a handful of the possible uses of paracord. You're going to want to have some on hand in a survival situation.

Rubber Bands

You can wrap a handful of rubber bands of various sizes around the outside of your tin. This will help keep your tin shut tight and it will allow you to keep some rubber bands on hand in case you need them without them taking up space in your tin.

You can use rubber bands for the following survival purposes:

- **An eraser.**
- **Can be wrapped around wound on fingers or toes and used as a bandage.**
- **Combine it with a stick to create a splint for a broken or sprained finger.**
- **Emergency tourniquets.**
- **Hold lids down tight.**
- **Hold your glasses onto your face.**
- **Lashing stuff together.**
- **Melt it and use it as adhesive.**
- **Pull long hair back.**
- **Thicker rubber bands can be combined with a forked stick to create a makeshift slingshot.**
- **Use it for diversionary purposes.** Shoot the rubber band at something in the opposite direction of where you're at. The noise may distract your pursuer enough to give you the upper hand.
- **Wrap around exposed wires to insulate against shock.**

- **Wrap rubber bands around a large stick to create a comfortable handle for a walking stick.**

Safety Pins

Toss a few safety pins of various sizes in your tin and you'll have a tool you can call on for all sorts of survival-related tasks. They're small and don't take up any space at all, so there's no good reason not to include a couple.

Here are just some of the many tasks you can accomplish using safety pins:

- **Can be used to cut paper.**
- **Drain blisters and boils.**
- **Emergency fishing hook.**
- **Hold papers together.**
- **Magnetize it and use it as a compass (see Navigation chapter).**
- **Make a makeshift sling by pinning the arm of a long sleeve shirt to the chest.**
- **Pick locks.**
- **Pin stuff up.**
- **Pin torn or tattered clothing together.**
- **Poke holes in stuff.**
- **Puncture tires on vehicles you don't want following you.**
- **Replace a missing button.**
- **Replacement zipper pull.**
- **Splinter removal.**
- **Stinger removal.**
- **Tighten the fit on loose-fitting clothing.**
- **Toothpick.**
- **Use to hold a large wound shut until you can get medical care.**

Another use for safety pins that most people wouldn't think of is as a makeshift weapon.

You may be able to conceal a large safety pin out of sight until the time is right. Aim for the eyes or the throat for maximum damage and shock value. If you plan on keeping a safety pin for defensive purposes, your best bet is to conceal a large safety pin somewhere on your clothing where it's unlikely to be found if you're searched by your captors. If you're captured, your survival tin is probably going to be confiscated.

Pocket Saw

The pocket saw is one tool that it's going to be tough to get by without. A pocket saw is a lightweight portable saw that consists of a chain with steel teeth on it that has handles attached to both ends. When you want to saw something, you grab the handles and run the saw back and forth across the wood you want to saw.

They work surprisingly well and can be used to cut firewood, branches and small trees for shelter and a number of other sawing tasks. For tougher sawing tasks, try attaching the handles to a curved piece of wood and using it like a hacksaw.

In addition to using your survival saw to cut wood, you can use it as a garrote if you need a makeshift weapon in a hurry. You're going to have to get up close and personal, but it's better than having nothing.

Small Multitool

A small foldable multitool is yet another tool that allows you to pack multiple tools into one small package. For your survival tin, a keychain-sized multitool is probably your best bet. On the other hand, you could opt to carry a full-size multitool in your pocket along with your kit.

A keychain multitool may contain the following tools:

- **Bottle opener.**
- **Can opener.**
- **Carabineer.**
- **File.**
- **Knife blade.**
- **Nail cleaner.**
- **Needlenose pliers.**
- **Regular pliers.**
- **Ruler.**
- **Scale.**
- **Scissors.**
- **Screwdriver.**
- **Tweezers.**
- **Wire cutters.**
- **Wire strippers.**

I'm partial to the Leatherman brand of multitool because they're built well and are hard to beat when it comes to functionality and quality. Don't go too cheap on your multitool. I've broken a number of cheaper tools from other brands in field testing. The Leatherman I bought many years ago when I first started prepping is still going strong.

Super Glue

Super glue is another one of those items you can include that don't take up much space and have a large number of uses. You can use super glue for the following survival tasks:

- **Binding wood together.**
- **Cover up fingerprints.**
- **Fire accelerant.**
- **Gluing stuff together.**
- **Patching holes in gear.**
- **Sealing minor cuts.**
- **Securing knots.**

Survival Cards

Survival cards are credit card-sized tools that are the thickness of 3 to 4 credit cards stacked on top of one another. These handy tools contain a number of tools inside them and make for efficient additions to your survival tin because they cover a lot of your needs in one small package.

You can find cards sold that contain at least some of the following tools:

- **Bottle opener.**
- **Can opener.**
- **Compass.**
- **Fire starter.**
- **Fixed-blade knife.**
- **LED flashlight.**
- **Magnifying glass.**
- **Ruler.**
- **Saw blade.**
- **Screwdriver.**
- **Toothpick.**
- **Tweezers.**
- **Whistle.**
- **Wrench.**

It's hard to argue that survival cards aren't a good choice when it comes to survival tins. They save space and allow you to carry a large number of tools in a space a little bigger than the size of a credit card.

Tampons

Believe it or not, tampons are probably one of the most useful items you can include in your survival tin. Get the bullet-type tampons and you'll be able to add a couple of them to your tin without taking up too much space. You'll be glad you did if you end up in an emergency situation.

Tampons can be used for the following things:

- **Feminine needs.**
- **Filter particles out of water.**
- **Fire tinder.**
- **Makeshift bandage.**
- **Plug wounds and bullet holes.**
- **Stop a bloody nose.**
- **Unravel and twist or braid the fibers to make string.**

Make sure you get tampons that aren't scented and don't have anything added. There's a rumor making the rounds on the Internet that some brands of tampons have anticoagulants in them and shouldn't be used in gunshot wounds. This simply isn't true. None of the major brands use anticoagulants, and I've yet to find *any brand* that uses them.

Navigation: Tools to Help You Find Your Way Home

When it comes to navigation, you're options are limited. You aren't going to have room for a handheld GPS unit, which is probably for the best, because it probably wouldn't work in a bad emergency anyway.

You also aren't going to have room to fold up a map and include it in your kit. You may be able to create a small map containing locations of potential sources of food and water in areas you're likely to be caught in if there's a catastrophe. You can include this as part of your information kit.

Be sure to identify landmarks that you'll be able to see from a distance. If you write on your map that a water hole is next to the small bronze statue in the park, you may or may not be able to locate it from a good distance away. On the other hand, if you indicate it's located next to the 3-story red and black parking garage, you'll be able to able to pinpoint the location from farther away.

Another navigation tool you're going to want in your kit is a button compass.

A cheap button compass can be purchased for less than 5 bucks. They're rather unreliable and won't work for long, if they work at all. Spend a little extra and get a good one and you'll have a compass that'll serve you well for quite some time.

I prefer the NATO survival compass (NSN 6605-99-522-0223) which is the size of a dime and is made of brass and glass. It's commonly used by the British Army and is designed to hold up under extremely harsh conditions. It's a bit more expensive than the cheaper plastic button compasses, but you can find one for less than $40 online.

If you're caught out without a compass, you can make one using a magnet, a needle and a piece of cork. Here are the instructions for making a magnet:

1. Slice off a coin-sized piece of cork.
2. Rub the magnet across the needle 15 times to magnetize the needle. Always rub it in the same direction.
3. Push the needle through the cork so equal parts of the needle stick out on both sides.
4. Fill a container with enough water to float the cork.
5. Set the cork in the water so it's floating on top and set the container on a flat surface.
6. The compass will point to whichever pole is closest. If you're closer to the North Pole it will point north. If you're closer to the South Pole, it will point south.

You can actually use anything that floats to create your compass. Place the item in the water and set the needle on top of it so equal parts of the needle hang off of both sides.
Here are some of the items I've seen used successfully:

- A leaf.
- A piece of dry cloth.

- A tire from a Matchbox car.
- Plastic milk carton cap.
- Sheet of plastic cut into a square.
- Styrofoam.

Signaling: It Might Just Save Your Life

You may find yourself in a situation where you're lost or injured and have to signal for help. Your cell phone could be lost, damaged or you might not have service to call for help—help that could be nearby, but unable to see you or hear your yells because you're just out of sight or they're looking in the wrong place.

Finding survivors is an imprecise science and you're going to want to up the odds that you'll be found as much as possible. The only way you're going to get found is through use of signaling.

Signaling is a form of communication that employs tools to call for help from much longer distances than you'd be able to without use of the tool. The ability to signal could be key to rescuers being able to find you in a disaster or emergency situation because your signal will reach much farther than your voice.

Here's a story that illustrates the importance of signaling.

Christian Johnson is an outdoors enthusiast. He lives close to the Adirondack Mountains and regularly goes on hiking trips there by himself. Much to his wife's chagrin, he often strikes off on trails through the mountains he discovers by chance, just to see where they take him. It's a passion of his and something he loves to do, to this very day.

One day Christian was driving through the mountains when he noticed a trail running off into the woods that he'd never taken before. He parked nearby and set off down the trail. He'd traveled a few miles when he came to a fork. The path on the left appeared to circle back in the direction he'd come, while the barely-existent path that went to the right appeared to make its way up the side of the mountain. Christian wasn't sure, but it looked like the path went all the way to the top. He decided he wanted to find out.

In a decision that would nearly cost him his life, Christian decided he wanted to see the view from the top and took the path to the right. The path meandered up the mountain, and Christian took his time scaling it. It was a steep and narrow path, but paths of this sort weren't anything new to Christian. In fact, he'd walked trails much more narrow and dangerous than this.

As he neared the top, the trail petered out, coming to an end abruptly just short of the top of the mountain. There were a couple large boulders blocking the path. The boulders rested against a sheer rock wall and were too big to scale. Christian's only choices were to turn around and head back or sidle past the boulders along the 6-inch lip of rock that jutted out over the edge of the cliff.

Christian assessed the situation.

He looked out over the trail he'd walked and mused at the fact he could see all the way down the mountain to the fork in the trail. He pondered turning around and walking back down. Then he turned his attention to the ledge. The 6-inch ledge looked solid. Looking over the edge, he found that he'd only fall 15 feet or so to another much larger ledge if he did fall, which may break a bone or two, but probably wouldn't kill him. He braced himself against the wall and sidled out along the ledge.

Luck wasn't with Christian this day.

He got halfway past the first rock and realized the ledge wasn't as wide as he'd originally thought. Even with his back pressed firmly against the boulder, half of each of his feet jutted out over the edge of the rock. A slight breeze was blowing, adding another layer of difficulty to the task at hand.

He slid his left foot along, testing each location by placing a bit of weight on it, and slid his right foot up to meet his left. Breathing deeply, he focused intently on moving and sliding, moving and sliding.

Reaching his right out again, Christian tested a spot and felt it shift just a bit under his weight. He stretched out even more and tested a spot further along the ledge. It felt solid, so he put his weight on it and started to slide his right foot up to the left. He felt the ledge start to give way and tried to pull back. His sudden movement threw him off-balance. He pin-wheeled his arms and tried to press his back against the boulder. Both feet slipped of the edge at the same time.

Christian doesn't remember the fall.

He snapped back to consciousness a while later, still waving his arms like he was teetering over the edge. It took him a moment to realize where he was. He'd fallen off the ledge! He took a moment to assess how badly hurt he was. He arms were bruised and scraped, but he was able to move them. His back hurt, but didn't seem to be broken or too badly damaged. He sat up to look at his legs and quickly realized how deep of trouble he was in. His left leg was fine. It was scraped up and his pants were torn, but it was none the worse for wear. His right leg had apparently absorbed most of the impact. It was twisted at an impossible angle and appeared to be broken in at least two places.

He wasn't going anywhere any time soon.

Christian's cell phone was in his pocket. He worked it out, trying not to move his damaged leg. It hurt while motionless. It screamed in agony with the least bit of movement. He managed to get his phone out of his pocket only to find the screen had been shattered in the fall and it was unusable. The screen lit up, but couldn't be read.

There wouldn't have been a signal anyway. He was just wondering what time it was. Judging by the way the sun was dancing behind the trees at the top of the ridge, Christian thought it was getting late.

He was *hoping* it was getting late. His wife would start to get worried when he didn't call and would contact authorities. She's already done it three times when his phone had died and he didn't have the charger with him in the car. He'd arrived home each time to an understandably angry Sheriff and an even angrier wife.

After promising he'd call on his way home *every single trip*, his wife forgave him and reluctantly agreed to let him continue with his little excursions.

Things went exactly as he thought they would.

His wife began to worry as the sun went down. When it had been down for an hour, she began to picture Christian dead at the bottom of a ravine. She called the authorities, who, considering their past history of false alarms, weren't exactly receptive to her pleas to send out a crew immediately. She then called as many of her friends and family members as she could round up and created a search party of her own.

The problem was they didn't know where to search. They knew the general direction Christian had headed, but didn't know exactly where he'd set off hiking. It took a couple hours just to find his vehicle.

By this time, it was starting to get cold and Christian was starting to get worried. The pain in his leg was so intense he was fading in and out of consciousness. He'd awake with a jerk, shivering in the biting cold until the pain became too much to bear and he passed out again. Each time he passed out, he stayed out for a little longer and it became harder for him to focus when he woke back up. He wasn't sure how much longer he was going to be able to hold on.

It took the search party an hour to get to the fork in the road. They looked at the trail that looped back around to the left and at the small trail that set off up the mountain to the right and decided only a madman would set off up such a dangerous looking trail on his own. They made the decision to follow the trail that looped back around in the direction from which they'd come.

As luck would have it, Christian snapped into reality as the search party reached the fork in the road. Through hazy vision he saw lights dancing around and wondered whether what he was seeing was real. The pain was intense, but he mustered all of his strength and started yelling. He might have well as been in a glass case. The wind picked up and carried his voice away long before it reached the bottom of the hill, let alone the search party at the fork.

In a blind panic, Christian looked for something he could throw. His hands scraped over the boulders around him and came to rest on something hard and plastic—his phone! In a flash of brilliance, Christian pressed the button on his phone and the light came on. He turned the light toward the search party and started waving it about in the air.

As they were turning to leave, an older teen boy in the party looked up the mountain to the peak. He saw a faint light flickering and almost dismissed it as his imagination. Instead, he tapped his dad on the shoulder and asked him if he saw the light, too. His dad saw it, and Christian was rescued from the mountain a couple hours later, exhausted and cold, but alive.

While Christian's leg was badly busted and he to this day doesn't have full use of it, he's alive and that's what matters. Alive because he was able to improvise and use his cell phone as a signal. This begs the question of what would have happened had the cell phone have been so badly damaged it didn't light up.

I'll tell you what probably would have happened. Christian would have died.

There are two types of signaling devices you can pack into your survival tin:

- **Those that rely on sight.**
- **Those that rely on sound.**

Visual signaling relies on catching the attention of the person or group you're trying to signal by using something that can be seen from a distance to call attention to the fact you need to be rescued. While rescuers may miss a tiny body on the side of a mountain (or may not be able to see the body at all, as is the case in the dark), it's tough to miss something that lights up or reflects sunlight.

When you're stranded in the dark—and to a lesser extent during the day—fire will attract attention from a good distance away. Your survival tin should have a source of fire in it anyway, and this source of fire can be used to create signal fires that will call attention to your location. The international distress signal is to build three fires in a triangle. Make sure you build them in an open area that can be seen from above. Aircraft passing by should see the fires and radio in that there's a person who needs help.

You can add to the effect by creating a larger fire onto which you throw large amounts of green moss and/or green leaves. This will create clouds of white smoke that will rise up into the air, making your position visible for miles.

Fire works great as a signal if you're stranded in the woods or out in the wilderness. It doesn't work so great if you're stranded in a building or in the city. If you're stuck on the upper floors of a skyscraper and there's a fire burning below you that you can't get past, you sure as heck aren't going to light the floor you're on aflame. You're going to want a signal that's less destructive.

You should also have a source of light in your emergency kit. Your light can serve double duty as a signal that you need help.

Use the light to send out an SOS distress call in Morse code when you see potential rescuers. The Morse code for SOS is as follows:

● ● ●　　　▬ ▬ ▬　　　● ● ●

Each of the dots represents a short pulse of the light. You can create a dot by quickly turning the light off and one. The dashes are created by leaving the light on for a longer period of time. Repeat the signal over and over again until the rescuers indicate they've seen you.

The last visual item you could opt to carry is a small signaling mirror. You aren't going to want to rely on the mirror as your only form of signaling because it won't work at night or on a cloudy day, but it can draw attention from miles away on a sunny day.

Most signaling mirrors are too big to add to a survival tin. They're too long and too wide and would take up too much space in your kit. If you want to add a signaling mirror to your kit, you're going to need to cut it down to a smaller size. Cut the mirror and drill a hole in the center that you can use for aiming. When you need to use the mirror, look through the hole and line up the reflected light of the sun with your target.

If you don't see anyone, don't give up. Sweep the mirror back and forth across the horizon until someone sees it and comes to help. Reflections from a signaling mirror can be seen for miles. Keep this in mind if you're using a signal mirror in a situation in which you want to stay hidden. Your signal mirror will give away your position if you don't aim it carefully.

Some people decide they don't want to carry a signal mirror in their kit. Instead, they polish the inside of their survival tin until it's highly reflective. This has the same effect as using a mirror—without having a mirror taking up valuable space.

When it comes to signaling using sound, you really only have one choice for your survival tin—the whistle. That's not to say there aren't a ton of whistles to choose from. There are, but you're pretty much limited to picking a whistle that suits your needs, unless you feel like carrying an air horn around in your pocket.

The best whistle I've found is the Extreme Cold whistle that's included in the USMC survival kit. This whistle is designed to work in sub-zero arctic conditions.

It's a flat whistle made from orange plastic that doesn't take up much space. It emits an ear piercing shriek that can be heard more than a mile away. You can find them on eBay from time to time for less than $5. Do a search for USMC Extreme Cold whistle or NSN# 8465-01-278-6982. The NSN number is the National Stock Number, which is the code the U.S. Government uses to order the whistle when it needs more.

The survival whistle works when visual signaling doesn't. It can be used any time of day and can help rescuers home in on you if you're trapped beneath rubble in a collapsed structure. They can also be used to help rescuers find you at night when there isn't a direct line of sight between you and your potential rescuers.

Putting It All Together

We've gone over a lot of items in this book. A whole lot. You'd need a kit the size of a lunchbox to store all of the items we've talked about.

Hey, there's an idea. The survival lunchbox. You could send your kids to school loaded down with gear to help them survive the schoolyard. Then again, you probably don't want your kids taking survival gear to school, especially not now that people are so hypersensitive to anything that has to do with prepping.

You aren't going to be able to fit everything you want into a kit the size of an Altoids can.

It isn't going to happen.

Instead, you're going to have to pick and choose the items you include. My tins (yes, I have multiple tins) contain at least one item from each of the categories, along with a few other small items I think might be helpful. I have multiple tins at the ready because I travel to different areas in both the city and the country and I like to have a separate kit outfitted for wherever I might be going.

Choose the items that are going to be the most useful to you. Don't pack stuff you aren't going to use or aren't willing to take the time to learn how to use before you need them.

If you've never set a snare before and don't think you could catch a squirrel if someone threw one at you, it's probably safe to assume including snare wire in your kit isn't going to help you any. Go heavier on the fishing stuff instead. You'll still be able to catch food, and that's what really counts. If you've attempted to start a fire with a fire striker and can't do it at home, you probably aren't going to be able to magically figure it out when your life depends on it. Bring other forms of starting fires with you. Lighters and matches will be your best friend in a survival situation.

These are just a couple examples of the decisions you're going to have to make. Pick tools that cover multiple items on the list in one small package to free up room for other stuff. It's a given you're going to have to pack light. There isn't any room for wasted space.

I'm constantly on the lookout for smaller or more efficient versions of the tools I have in my tin(s). I'm also constantly moving things in and out of my tin(s) as I discover new items. Don't set and forget the items in your tin. Keep it up to date make sure you know the items that are in there inside and out.

Contact Me

Questions? Want more info? Have an item you include in your tin that I didn't mention? Feel free to contact me at the e-mail address listed below. Be patient, as I get a lot of e-mails. I try to answer all of them, so if you don't get an answer in a few days, try resending your message in case it fell through the cracks.

Here's the address you can contact me at:

miklanderson2@yahoo.com

Additional Reading Material

If you enjoyed this book and want to read more interesting survival books, the following books may be right up your alley:

Bugging In: How to Hunker Down and Survive in an Emergency Situation

http://www.amazon.com/dp/B00C5PEQVM

Want to learn how to hunker down and survive in your home in a shelter-in-place situation? While bugging out gets all the media attention, bugging in is probably your best bet for survival. Learn why and learn how to survive in your home in this new book by author M. Anderson.

The Poor Man's Prepping Guide: How to Prepare for Disaster on a Shoestring Budget

http://www.amazon.com/dp/B00C3Y0K92

The Poor Man's Prepping Guide is the perfect book for the prepper looking to get prepared for disaster on a minimal budget. Can you afford not to be prepared when disaster strikes?

The Bug Out Bag: What You Need to Stay Alive

http://www.amazon.com/dp/B00AI2UF1Y

Got a bug out spot all picked out that you plan on packing up and heading to when things go bad? You're going to need a bug out bag to help get you there. This book will teach you to pack your bug out bag the right way, so it's full of items that are going to help you stay alive when you bug out.

Seed Saving for the Organic Gardener

http://www.amazon.com/dp/B00B73O7GW

Saving seeds is something every prepper should know how to do. Martin Anderson's comprehensive new guide gives you the information you need to get started saving seeds.